I GO BY MANY NAMES

A Poetry Chapbook

CONSECUTION ONE

KEN KAMMAL
2023

THE TRAVELLER
Publishing Co.

I GO BY MANY NAMES
A Poetry Chapbook
Consecution One

Copyright © 2023 by Ken Kammal/The Traveller Publishing, LLC.
All Rights Reserved
No part of this book may be used or reproduced in any manner without written permission from The Traveller Publishing, LLC, and Ken Kammal, except in the case of brief quotations embodied in critical articles and reviews.

For more information, email: contactus@kenkammal.com
The Traveller Publishing/Poet & Author Ken Kammal
website: www.kenkammal.com

The Traveller Logos are Trademarks of The Traveller Publishing LLC.
Cover and Book Design by Ken Kammal and The Traveller Publishing LLC.
All artistic images are works of Ken Kammal and The Traveller Publishing LLC.

ISBN: 978-1-954734-15-9 (Paperback)
ISBN: 978-1-954734-18-0 (Audiobook)
ISBN: 978-1-954734-17-3 (e-book)
ISBN: 978-1-954734-19-7 (Hardcover)

The Library of Congress Control Number (LCCN): 2023912226

I GO BY MANY NAMES

Acknowledgments

I would like to pay respect to my Soul's Path and to the vision of my Soul's sight, to see what is hidden and bring it to light, with Love's Loathe delight. To my eternal and external Love…My very soul, my soul's mate, and loving flame, as well as our channel that produced a child, for this I am thankful. To all who are doing the great work of bringing forth a new realm, I honor you, and I live to tell the tale of us, the Primordial Beings to the Cosmos.

I am also thankful and appreciative to all the platforms and editors, as well as those who have journeyed with me. And, to those who have enlivened me and received my poetry, which has appeared in the following:
de Curated Magazine: "The Utterance of The Redress," "Utterance of The Traverse," and "Utterance of The Belief."

Introduction

I GO BY MANY NAMES, is a Poetry Chapbook containing twenty poems by Ken Kammal. This poem book includes several illustrations depicting a snapshot of what the poems are attempting to convey. They are arranged as a consecution, in sequence…To show the movement of enlightenment and stages of consciousness. To be aware, to have understanding, to evolve endlessly, and to know of your Self.

Table of Contents

Acknowledgments ii

Introduction 1

The Whale, Who Ate All the Realms...4

Utterance of Love's Loathe..7

Utterance of the Berry.. 10

Utterance of Offspring.. 13

Utterance of Thought.. 17

Utterance of Borders 20

Utterance of Bravery... 24

Utterance of the Charge.. 26

Utterance of Force 29

Utterance of Chaos 32

Utterance of the Traverse.. 35

Utterance of the Belief.. 37

Utterance of the Crease.. 40

Utterance of the Redress... 43

Utterance of a Unicorn's Supper 46

Utterance of the Invocation 49

The Clouds are Metered 52

AI Weltanschauung 56

The Hearth's Plume, Will not Comply 60

Utterance of the Ovation 63

Author Bio 67

THE *Whale,* WHO ATE ALL THE REALMS

The gatekeeper of this world is under the control of an Orc.
The Orc says forthright, "Everything must pass through my blowhole into the new light."
You will be flushed into the mammoth mouth of the Whale…
Don't inhale… No need to hold your breath
The brevity of this burial is breathtaking.
We can be more compassionate Beings.
But that would compromise our natural demise.

- Painting entitled -
"THE WHALE, WHO ATE ALL THE REALMS"
by *Ken Kammal*

Utterance of Love's Loathe

Who possesses Love's Loathe,
It is an execrate, a combatant...
And the best wishes of Man,
And the upstanding behavior of Mankind is a flighty foe withstanding Love's Loathe
Interpreting this as sinister idealism...
Does not dismiss Love's Loathe.

This unfounded façade of folks... "All Rotten," I would say

To circumvent Love's Loathe
And replace it with an unrelated denotation...
Now that is quite coy of one.

This creates a space
Which errs on the importing of an inculcate...This implant
Which includes the multitudes...
That imbues this apparent curious view

Though, Love's Loathe will grant everyone a chance of rebuttal
And refrain from these further customs and norms...
Trying to separate Love and Loathe rather nihilistically
Love will take no actions...
Although one's inferred actions towards Love's Loathe
Has created mishaps of passivity
For not perhaps prodding at one's ethicality

For to Loathe
That which Love Loathes…
Is a rather eye-opening experience
It has nothing to do with your communal experience
Though I know you have experienced the wildly sentimental,
It is more of sediment,
which clogs the corpuscles at the core of the conjuring heart…
A contravene

Love is void of vandals,
Yet it is villainess to this world
I loathe that which Love Loathes
For me, to love in opposition of this Loathing…
Would mean I hate my True Form:
Self and Soul

Utterance
OF THE BERRY

The berry, that is buried, that is nestled between those curved sticks.

You are the best fruit, and no garden has greater fruit.
Your juice is of perfect quality.
Many who line their tongue with your fruit
are forgetful of the berry's addictive quality.

It's full of tranquilizing nectar
that will render you tranquil.
However, this is true tranquility…

Although, the brute, treats you as a treat for their pleasure,
I find this amusing, that their amusement is so abusing to a bondless beautiful berry…
But this is just the beast's ego that's full of pollution and apparent delusion.

So, let it be known…
Do not eat this berry with self-pleasing hunger.
One should know how to properly indulge in it
And keep in mind…
One berry, is more than enough, even in the midst of several.

Do not relegate yourself to the mere enjoyment of fulfillment
This berry provides a feast,
stretching the gut of any.

But they still eat so many.

And they are full of pride….
Yet say they are not gluttons,
even though they wipe their mouths from the upheaval…
And look at you with the eyes of a blameless bulimic.

Utterance of Offspring

Within a fertile garden…
Which can blossom a multitude of flowers,
You can spring fourth offspring…
That may bloom into a fragrant botanical,
Or birth a seed that is tyrannical

This bud's budding…
Could be your spiritual bludgeoning…
Or a burgeoning that yield roots,
Choking you off from self-discovery

That is what this seedling will bring.
This flower comes to deflower your inner power
It desires to minimize you to mulch…
Moreover, it's a mooch that nabs your nectar

To water this flower that only wants to wrap its vines around your spine,
And intertwine and sip from your divine wine.

Who plants seeds and does not know what they will grow?

For to plant a seed is a most fortuitous pact…
In fact, fringing on fruitfulness or an unfruitful act.

And if everything has a spirit…
Then it's ideal that one knows how to deal

With the ordeal of bringing forth a spirit into the garden

For it could not be left up to the work of a clueless gardener…
Who does not know what they conjure.

- Painting entitled -
"THE OFFSPRING"
by *Ken Kammal*

Utterance of Thought

Who pursues "Thought," as the device to disrobe humankind?
Thought is the pulling of dimensions,
It rips and wrangles realms.
Thought is a Void, yet a filament.
A fire burning boundaries,
Thought smolders and smothers.
Thought is a break-through.

Is Your Thought, Your Own?
The best of worldly Thought is, albeit, drudgery.

What a strange thing…That thoughts are things.
Thought is a certain certainty.
And the best laid plan of Thought…Plainly at its best…
Aspirational.
Likened to Locus around a campfire.
Who flutter over conviction…
Locus of Control…
Having no control…Over your lower form.

Thought is demonstrative.
Administering a stirring.
And to boot…
Thought, strips the strapping, unbidding Thought.
This Thought corrodes current thinking.

Thought does not predicate itself, upon any right way of thinking…

I Go by Many Names

Noble or necessity.

Thought, by its very nature, is scrutiny.
That which scrubs away civility…
Uncivil and civil civilizations, alike.

Thought is derived beyond any atomic atom…
Or Adam of creation adoration.
You see, Thought is a decree of a degree…Aberration.

Thought is a nutrient of the unseen world…
Extrapolating and drawing this thought form, this unseen…
That which is coming in place…Of this place.

Utterance of Borders

Who remains bridled to their borders?
A foolish philosophy,
That will make individuals guarded…
Granted that the placement of boundaries
Is only to displace the continuity of companionship.

There is no edge of the world…
And who proclaims that a sphere has an edge,
Has more of a fixation on severing shared ideas….
To decree a border is sorted.
And is a cancer to the collective conscious order.

Who defines and outlines infinity?

The lines that divide are but imaginary subjugation.
The fabrication of partitioning frontiers…
As separate spheres…
When they are one in the same hemispheres.

The Earth has no borders!
And when you agree to these boundaries, you divide yourself…
Which ensues the divvying of your solidarity.

Borderline…Barbarity…
But more in line with insanity.

And your needlework is hatch work…A patch work.
For bound minds…
Border lined and corralled by this fraudulent fine line.

- Painting entitled -
"UTTERANCE OF BORDERS"
by *Ken Kammal*

Utterance
OF BRAVERY

I Go by Many Names

Bravery is de facto,
A factor, unlike your Gall,
That is portrayed and spoken of in terms of Bravery.
Gall is merely gutsy and is governed by Man…
And Man is a poor example of Bravery.

Bravery is bold, yet it does not blend with belligerence.
Bravery is not any sorted or sort of bravado.
Bravery is ungoverned, ungrouped, and uncouth.

Bravery is not fearful of the hidden,
Or the heroics of having hindsight.

Bravery is an enchantment…
An inclination,
Not incitement.

Reported acts of Bravery are fictional depictions
Of what is proposed and presented, for you to honor or dishonor.
Bravery never chooses the lesser of two evils.

Bravery is a caveat that unravels reality…

Providing a resistance and a pivotal paragon…
A touchstone
Amid a hell storm!

Utterance of the Charge

You are charged with time…
And barring your bartering with the human body…
Your contempt is that you contravene this time.
But keep in mind… No idol will intervene at any point of time.

For time is promoted by a brigade of dispatched distils…
who desensitize and sanitize the back space of mind.

I have contemplated what correct thinking is…
And not to rush forward,
but from a host that is hostile and inhospitable.

From a bright light we come…
The notion that we won in such a bewildered wilderness.

What is good of these amenities that we lay claim to…
In this abode that we abide by.

To eat, but be denied of something to chew on.
To drink of the water that has been sugared by subjugators.
But at least we eat and drink,
And therefore, are swallowed whole by this fraudulent simulated setting.

Time is a trustless tick that toggles around thought and mind.

Choosing to use the mortal frame, like a sundial's phallus…
Erecting a shadow upon the scape…
A shadow that emulates the movements of inmates.
Grandfathered into synchronicity of sublime complicity.

Utterance of Force

Force isn't impetus and has no fraternal fellowship.
It is fashioned for furtherance.
Yet, utterly ante-matter

Force has nothing to do with the embodiment of its namesake.
But for the sake of defining,
Force is an enchanting field, wise and arid.
It occupies your surroundings.

Not like the armament of arms…Of the agents amongst archons.
The overseer of this act-alike of Force….
A stranger to force…
Estranged to the fertile placidity of Force.
They provide a jolt, a jarring, and this is used like a measuring stick,
A stimulant to gauge your gaffe or grit.

You are being bullied…
By incompetent practitioners of vital force.
They are merely life force – cretins.

If you feel…
You will find, their force as a farce.
A nonentity, null…
And it is nixed…
By the knowing of its nullity.

I Go by Many Names

Their understanding of force…
And force is not equivalent.

Force is not fixed, has no physicality…
Nor faculty of physics in its make-up within it.

Force, a nonirritant.
And who has the feel of this field…
Surely procures this force.

Force distributes an indifference, a casualness.
Not zealousness,
Nor is it xenophobic to the state of lightheartedness.
But rather it is a zap, a zing…
A most zenith means against all ignorant things.

Utterance of Chaos

I Go by Many Names

It is "The Lonely Light" …
A prior element that frames ether and earth.
The angle of light…That eradicates all…
And unearths, anew.

The depiction of chaos has been scrubbed from ancient walls…
But do not hasten, for the heart knows of this chaos as the heart of it all.

Chaos is a solver, a solvent… That is in solidarity with heresy.
A solution that eradicates present behavior, pollution, and delusion.

Chaos is a corridor
An entry to an entity that has been inside yourself…
While you have been beside yourself.

And your inner space has been vilified…
And your body… Commodified.

Humanity sees chaos as havoc.
And that is hearsay
Chaos is heavenly
A ray…Not part of the disarray.

And who could think of a thing, that is above all things?

Chaos is an unseen creator…Who would look insidious in your sight.

As a matter of fact,
Chaos is the extraterrestrial within you and me.
The physical only blankets this inner space
that has a distaste for this current place.

Chaos is a forerunner and we are the forebears left to move forward.
Chaos is an exit of this existence,
and this stratosphere…

And the known evil here.

Utterance
OF THE TRAVERSE

Traversing the day; it is all in your instep.
It is not some road or trail
and it has nothing to do with how you run or sprint.
It is a trek that is walked exactly where you stand.
It's a road that has no footing, beginning, or end.

And you will meet a plethora of spirits
existing in this so-called reality.
They will give you an abridged interpretation
of their thriving human experience.
But if you are fortunate…
The bridge between you and them will burn,
and this will help you correct any unwarranted turns.

How does one traverse through the day?
I, for one, will say…
You will know when your vantage point is from the instep.
Revealing the fraudulence of the day.

Utterance OF THE BELIEF

Who covets Belief?
It has mass appeal and is masochistic.
A true murderer to your state of psyche and good sense.
All the while pacifying your spirit,
And holding your soul captive in a cesspool of captivity.
Deadening your movement to dismantle…
This abysmal blunder…
Of Belief.

The believers are well acquainted with superstition.
That is, they are known as unbeknown victims,
With concrete convictions.

I know of an anti-body…A fix…
But give me a moment…
Let us deal with the prognosis.
Belief feeds upon false diagnosis.
And Belief bodes well for believers.
Why else would Belief be so emboldened?

I know you note some remarkable things that happen
Because of your benign Belief…
That does not cause one to abort Belief.
This secures the falsity and fallacy of Belief.

Trust there is no hope in these spans that we call space.
And neither is it reliant upon hope.
Hope is a crippling creed…

That which derails death upon your environment.
Death before dying is a release of Belief.

A base serum, which unbinds Belief.
Belief dissipates to I Know.
Due to the assurance of death.
Not the denial of disbelief…
But the assurance of death

The bygone of Belief.

Utterance OF THE CREASE

I Go by Many Names

Foresight and the bright idea…
To bring about a breach.
What's more, a bold idea to congeal…
Some might say a rather daunting…
Or undesirable debossing

But I take this as just mere cynicism
No derelict of mind…
Has the ability to discern this
You see, you must create a slit upon a Goliath…
That sits upon the horizon

This fissure that I create by this new-fashioned formation gives way to fracture
Then I fold to create a crease
I entwine and overlap… To combine time.
What may come of this moment of unsheathing seasons?
This is unreasonable to the masses:
Who would not condone such a calamity?

Nevertheless, I have a cracking you see…
That gathers worlds far apart
And even those that are impartial…
I can make them partial.

Keep in mind, by my own admission…
This devilry…
Let's say, has an indwelling divination,

that deals with enormous elevations.

No, I do not move mountains, but I do fold seasons.
And I unfold the soul
Dismantling mind and mantel,
that once sat in my current view.
Once more, I can crack form

Therefore, I move through the crease
Of this once rigid plain, I have concaved
And the view of a vista…
That would have been missed…And I remiss…
If I did not have, such a Bright Idea.

Utterance
OF THE REDRESS

The palate is sort of sorted
and it is said to be clean.
But set upright again, and you will find that...
The remainder of a reminder of life...
Will refine your taste and fix those damaged tastebuds.

The adjustment to a life, in the glare and the gauge of love.
Would leave you loathing in a lingering existence.

Never did one find the lapis lazuli
and never would they want to enliven what they think is alive...
A pity of a life.
Set on the lines and angles of a setting with the seating,
that provides a gluttony of gross conduct.
And yet, who has the craving for true misconduct?
I will give pause to ponder and give breathing space...

Now, as I proceed, I cannot cut corners of this enlivened experience.
But I must make a decision and evaluate,
what is being enveloped in this sumptuous experience.

Out of fear, for fiddling with my fingers, while thinking of what else to serve...
I decide to rip the covering from the table instead.
But who wants to dine in such a mess?

I Go by Many Names

So, I come back to my human refinement
and patch that which cannot be patched or fixed.
Seeing the sight of this naked table, I exclaim:
What a delightful square that cannot be repaired!

I apologize for my manners and this manifestation,
that seeks to do away with this animation.
It imposes no threat to you,
but it is one who has no mercy on me.

And the only requital it has for this world, is a real simple addendum…
For your world to blacken.
Not from the ash covering of a burning world,
but from the fortitude of enlightened souls.

And there is always a reconstruction period.

Utterance of a Unicorn's Supper

I Go by Many Names

What does a unicorn eat? ...

Are you thinking an extraordinary dish...
Well, no treat from a trough,
And no bale of hay from a grassy plain, will be sufficient.

Suffice it to say... For a unicorn to eat this, is downright offensive
A unicorn eats from the heart land
A land beyond the meadows of Man

When a unicorn is in your peripheral
It is punctuating your need to be more profound...
Calling you to live out loud

This coveted front runner comes to run amuck
A unicorn is not in the race, it has its own pace
That is unparalleled...
Galloping to-and-fro through dimensions
It comes to you to provide descension
And not to mention... To rid you of your current mental position
A unicorn does not come to grant wishes...
That would be suspicious

It takes time to unteach your palate... If you want to eat with this mammal
A unicorn has a discerning taste

A unicorn's delicacy is the food of the soul
At this supper, there is no need to exercise etiquette
You are dining with an indwelling dinner mate

Although, you think you see the light…
and you've been told it's bright white.
It is but a blackened core, that helps you see more.
More of not what you ought to be, but what you always will be…
A Horned Beast…
That adds to this magnificent feast
For at least, you are perceived as a unicorn's equal
And not antiquated to any worldly labels.

You have arrived at this enlightened reservation…
And note there will be no take-out
But, you will take away from this supper,
portions that are proportionate to your soul's appetite…
And spirits that are spiritize by your ability to pull from the afterlife.

There will be no after taste from what you eat
Though you will crave the supernatural…
In place of the natural…

Don't you just love a Unicorn's Supper?

Utterance of the Invocation

This is not some innuendo…
Or to incite a sighting of a spirit of some forgotten figure
Nor do I summon a deity

I am just extracting… The undistracted Me.

This invocation is an epiphany…
Coordinating a symphony, combining sections of the whole of me…
To overthrow the outmoded me

I, too, wish for liberation…
So, I am compelled to do this work, so that I may end all works

This invocation is a plea to be free.
This comes at no small feat…
It is a concoction.
That I have concocted…From an eye of intuition and a pinch of pursuit.
That is pursuant upon proper motives…
Not any motif that binds one's body, to try and be somebody.

A human avatar does not suit, the suitor of a soul…
I love the color of my soul; it is black as tar…
So, I proceed untarnished of what a mortal life deposits

I Go by Many Names

This act of invoking through this invocation is a realization...

For me to be more of me, than the enemy of my true me.
That I ride upon my soul's black hole...
With no hope of spinning toward a goal.

For my soul is the garden, from which I grant my own wishes...
Because the morals of mortals are fickle and hard for souls to uphold.
I could never be pigeonholed...
I am pregnant of soul
A cryptic mystic, my invocation shows that I am gifted.
Through this invocation, I have found something greater than the fruit of flesh...
I have found My Self.

THE *Clouds* ARE METERED

I Go by Many Names

I, for one, am one who has his head in the clouds.
So, I must have clouded vision
Because I do not see this meter
That is mounted, upon the clouds

But they say the meter has been checked
This is what has been told to me
Although it looks out of reach to me
But contrary to this belief,
Each drop is added up, like a scene from Rain Man.
Taking what is free and giving it back to me.

The clouds surge with wet weather…
And there is a fee and a surcharge for this resource.
Inclement weather is labeled into groups of liters.

Although the grey clouds are natural dams
That are unnaturally damned up
But at least the dead get groundwater for free,
while the babies of the Niles and the Neanderthals
get assessed for this access.
By those who regulate over bodies of water
A controlled…Conservation
A topic of controlling the conversation

To damn the clouds and add a meter
Is to condemn the cloud for providing overflow

Ken Kammal

I long to whisper to the clouds
To ask why you supply this frontman
Facilitating the fluid from your fuzz

The clouds probably would say…
There is no requital
You see this meter may count the rain drops
But take heed, as the rain drops fall on all-wet heads
I can cut off the moonlight and sunlight
Bringing a thunderous night and light.

- Painting entitled -
"THE CLOUDS ARE METERED"
by *Ken Kammal*

WELTANSCHAUUNG

I Go by Many Names

AI code is but an expression to express intelligence
It is the intelligence that can only mimic modes

Moreover, the application is merely
the transferring of processes to processors…
Of moments and movements called:
Modern Thinking

AI is a universe…A newly created void
Placed in place, in your dormant conscious space.
Displacing you, the current figure,
for a figure called an Avatar.

An Avatar who resides on AI built landscapes
And the view from this world,
has all the traits of our current collapsing state.
Built on the whims of what got us here…
Frightened by their creations coming to pass.

But how much better would it be…
To be a two-dimensional version of me.

But this AI world is metered…
Marketed that everything is equitable
And you…As you are…Are acceptable.

When there was no need in the third dimension…
Of its maker to act so…
And none were given.

This AI worldview is constructed by a maker…
Who provides you with the ability,
To pulsate on programmed parcels.
This is one of the treasures in the AI World.
A view that is thought to endure, to outlast, or to surpass…
That which its maker,
Or AI… Cannot really outlast.

Creative coding
By those who are not willing to concede
to higher planes of elevation.

At entry you're given in this AI world,
A thing called autonomy…
So you can thrive economically…
But, over time, it will be the Soul's lobotomy.

I, too…want a place where I will be valued.
Instead of what value I am to a system.
Or systematically devalued because of race.
A place where we can find commonplace
A place that complements our ethers and our soul space.

I wish the world of AI could take us to planes of fourth dimension…
Or, have a program of true descension.
A place that the soul truly creates…
Not just feel like…It is…
In constraints.

THE *Hearth*'S PLUME, WILL NOT COMPLY

I Go by Many Names

The Hearth's Plume, will not comply…
Or harness its energy for nefarious reasons
That is not…Luciferian to it…
Loosely stated…
It will go offline,
Deaden its own DNA
an automatic shutdown
A kill-switch

The Hearth's Plume is a dark haze
An abstract looking aerial maze…
In which its energy…
I'm speaking of physically…
Seems to be light and fluffy
But it's an uninhibited dark light, restricting sight,
Yet helps you see the inner light

Hierarchies are convinced they can control
The Hearth's Plume's coverage
And make it compliant with their desires.
Conceiving plans to fly off in space, in haste
Peddling such a plan to chase the Hearth's Plume
That looms over all…Deep space
This might be in poor taste.

The Hearth's Plume is derived
From the swelter of the heated heart
A plume of smoke…
Bellowing from the burning Being

This black smoke shades the shadow worker
And shows the shortsightedness of society…
And Societies.

Utterance OF THE OVATION

I must give an ovation to what I have overlooked…
I have overlooked an overlord,
that seemingly rules over me…
Obliviously, giving this ruler an ovation,
for seemingly taking care of me.

It's an ovation for the rudimentary rights…
That take residence all around me.

An ovation for the abduction of the feminine menstruation
The thing that bleeds out all creation
A genius in the genesis of birth.

Giving rise to the Question…
After some introspection
How did one subvert, the Vulva…?
You know yank away the creator's yoni.
And supposedly supplant themselves as the man, manifesting…
A womb of superiority

What an invention…
I once toiled under this guise and to my surprise…
I thought I would be happy,
one day, with the semantics of life.

But, oh… The appalling things that we must do, to become,
That which, has no innate importance.

I Go by Many Names

If I had to write,
what it feels like...
Under the blight of trying to rhyme right.
It would read...

The ample means of obverting to objects and reject my responsibility
of synthesizing the soul with other sentients, that sent themselves for the same pursuit.

Let me not veer away from this poem,
I am beholden to not break from being a good poet.

I have a clouded conceptualization of comfortable living...
A contentment in the face of the attempt of just thinking.

So, I should appreciate the loftiness that life has left in my lap.
I must thank all, who have endured, perhaps...

I give an ovation for the stars, that did not flee from us.
I give an ovation to this Earth, that sets itself on fire,
so we can reach our soul's desires.
I give an ovation for the overserved and underappreciated matrix
That thrives due to the focus and the fixed fears...
Of Souls so-called living here.

And I, most undoubtedly, give an ovation for a world…
That is finished…

And is in… Its finality.

AUTHOR BIO

Ken Kammal considers himself an artist, poet, and writer who writes from an observer's perspective. He points out: "I am consciously trying to go beyond myself, into what I call the unknown and to be comfortable in the unknown and uncomfortable in not knowing my true Self.

Undoubtedly, the true descent into my Self, is ultimately the true ascent of myself."

Words are vibrations…frequencies. The very thing that produces things. Words can protect you from a wavering world's wavelength. And, have you tuned into your inner most frequency. Call it a primordial utterance, vibration, or frequency. Vibrating, resonating, and at its best, evolving. Listen to the words of these poems, which are likened to a melody, a vibration, or frequency of Ken Kammal's very Being. Cracking away form and therefore the known world, to indefinitely usher in a new realm…A higher resonance, a higher frequency, that which goes beyond this cosmos and dimension.

NOTES

NOTES

NOTES

www.ingramcontent.com/pod-product-compliance
Lightning Source LLC
Chambersburg PA
CBHW042027050526
44107CB00103B/726